Mammals

Jinny Johnson
Consultant: Steve Parker

Miles Kelly
PUBLISHING

First published in 2002 by
Miles Kelly Publishing Ltd
Bardfield Centre, Great Bardfield, Essex, CM7 4SL

Copyright © Miles Kelly Publishing 2002
2 4 6 8 10 9 7 5 3 1

Some material in this book can also be found in *100 Things You Should Know About Mammals.*

Editor: Amanda Learmonth

Design: Debbie Meekcoms

Assistant Editor: Nicola Sail

Index: Lynn Bresler

Art Director: Clare Sleven

British Library Cataloguing-in-Publication Data
A catalogue record for this book is available from the British Library

ISBN 1-84236-109-0

Printed in Hong Kong

www.mileskelly.net
info@mileskelly.net

ACKNOWLEDGEMENTS

The Publishers would like to thank the following artists who have contributed to this book:

Chris Buzer (Studio Galante), Luca di Castro (Studio Galante), Jim Channell (Bernard Thornton Illustration), Mike Foster (Maltings Partnership), Wayne Ford, Chris Forsey, L.R. Galante (Studio Galante), Brooks Hagan (Studio Galante), Emma Louise Jones, Roger Kent, Stuart Lafford (Linden Artists), Kevin Maddison, Alan Male (Linden Artists), Janos Marffy, Massimiliano Maugeri (Studio Galante), Colin Newman (Bernard Thornton Illustration), Eric Robson (Illustration Ltd), Mike Saunders, Francesco Spadoni (Studio Galante), Christian Webb (Temple Rogers)

Computer-generated artwork by James Evans

Contents

What are mammals? **4**

The world of mammals **6**

Tallest and smallest **8**

Top racers **10**

High fliers **12**

River mammals **14**

Snow mammals **16**

In the jungle **18**

Desert life **20**

City life **22**

Plant-eaters **24**

Hungry hunters **26**

Fins and flippers **28**

Champion diggers **30**

Staying safe **32**

Best builders **34**

Getting at food **36**

Baby mammals **38**

Index **40**

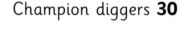

What are mammals?

Mammals are warm-blooded animals with a bony skeleton and fur or hair. Being warm-blooded means that a mammal can keep its body at a constant temperature, even if the weather is very cold. There is one sort of mammal you know very well – you!

African savanna elephant

Eurasian beaver

Meerkat

Eurasian otter

Cheetah

Red panda

Greater
fruit bat

**The Eurasian
otter**
has webbed
feet to help
it swim.

Lion

Western tarsier

Meerkats
live together in
family groups.

Greater
horseshoe bat

Raccoon-dog

**The Western
tarsier**
sleeps during
the day and
hunts at night.

5

The world of mammals

There are nearly 4500 different types of mammal. Most have babies which grow inside the mother's body. While a baby mammal grows, a special organ called a placenta supplies it with food and oxygen from the mother's body. These mammals are called placental mammals.

▲ Olive baboons live in Africa in groups called troops of between 20 and 150 animals.

◀ Marsupials give birth to young that finish growing in a pouch. The tiny baby kangaroo makes its own way to the safety of its mother's pouch, where it begins to feed on a teat.

The echidna is one of two groups of mammals that lays eggs instead of giving birth.

Bats are the only mammals that are able to fly.

Bernie's fun facts!

Bears love honey. They tear bees' nests apart to get at the honey – but don't seem to mind getting stung!

▲ The fallow deer, like all deer, has a good sense of smell. This is so that it can sniff the air for the scent of an enemy.

Tallest and smallest

The blue whale is the biggest mammal. It spends all its life in the sea. It can measure more than 33.5 metres long – that is as long as seven family cars parked end to end. The elephant is the biggest land mammal, while the smallest mammal in the world is the tiny hog-nosed bat.

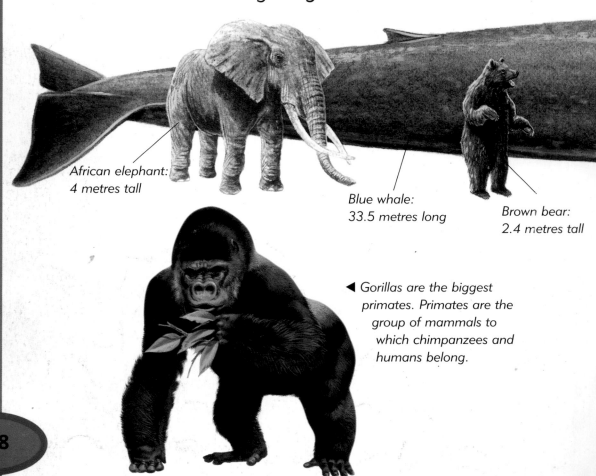

African elephant: 4 metres tall

Blue whale: 33.5 metres long

Brown bear: 2.4 metres tall

◀ Gorillas are the biggest primates. Primates are the group of mammals to which chimpanzees and humans belong.

▶ The tiny hog-nosed bat is only three centimetres long. It weighs only two grams – less than a teaspoon of rice!

The mouse deer is the smallest deer – it is only the size of a hare.

Human: 1.7 metres tall

Giraffe: 5.5 metres tall

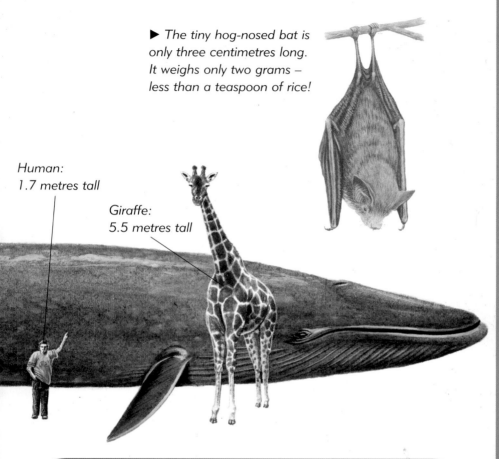

The capybara is the largest rodent. Rodents are the group that includes rats and mice.

Test your memory!

1. How many types of mammal are there?

2. Where does a baby kangaroo finish growing?

3. Which is the only mammal that can fly?

4. What is the special organ that supplies food and oxygen to a baby mammal in the mother's body?

1. nearly 4500 2. in its mother's pouch 3. the bat 4. the placenta

The pygmy shrew is the smallest land mammal.

9

Top racers

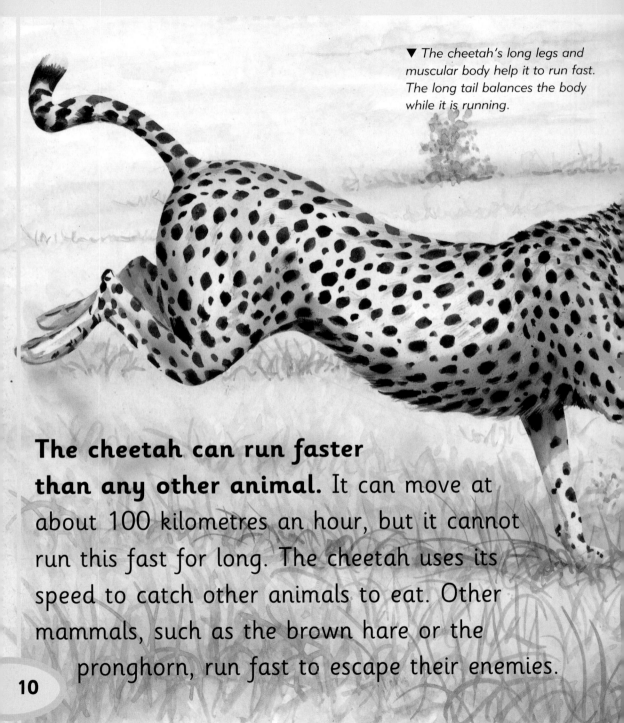

▼ *The cheetah's long legs and muscular body help it to run fast. The long tail balances the body while it is running.*

The cheetah can run faster than any other animal. It can move at about 100 kilometres an hour, but it cannot run this fast for long. The cheetah uses its speed to catch other animals to eat. Other mammals, such as the brown hare or the pronghorn, run fast to escape their enemies.

The pronghorn is one of the fastest mammals in North America.

The brown hare has strong back legs to help it move quickly.

The red kangaroo is a champion jumper.

Speed demons!

How do you compare to the fastest mammal on Earth?

1. Ask an adult to help. Measure how far you can run in 10 seconds. Times this by 6.

2. Times the answer by 60. This will tell you how many metres you can run in an hour.

3. Divide this by 1000. You will get your speed in kilometres per hour. You will find it will be far less than the cheetah's 100 kilometres per hour!

High fliers

Bats are the only true flying mammals. They zoom through the air on wings made of skin. Flying lemurs don't really fly — they just glide from tree to tree. Other gliding mammals are flying squirrels and gliders.

Fruit-eating bats feed mostly on fruit and leaves.

Vampire bats feed only on the blood of other mammals!

▲ Lemurs and flying squirrels glide from tree to tree with the help of flaps of skin at the sides of their body.

Bernie's fun facts!

A vampire bat drinks about 26 litres of blood a year. That's about as much as the total blood supply of five human beings!

River mammals

Most river mammals spend only part of their time in water. Creatures such as the river otter and the water rat live on land and go into the water to find food. The hippopotamus, on the other hand, spends most of its day in water to keep cool.

▶ The river otter's ears close off when it is swimming. This stops water getting into them.

Eurasian otter

Test your memory!

1. What is the biggest land mammal?
2. What kind of mammal is a capybara?
3. Which mammal can run the fastest?
4. What do vampire bats feed on?

1. the elephant 2. a rodent 3. the cheetah 4. blood

14

▼ The Ganges dolphin is blind. It uses sound waves to find food. The waves bounce off the food telling the dolphin where to find it.

The platypus uses its duck-like beak to find food in the riverbed.

Manatees are water-living mammals that feed on plants.

▼ Webbed feet make many water creatures good swimmers.

Water rat

The hippo is not a good swimmer, but can walk on the riverbed.

Water opossum

15

Snow mammals

The polar bear is the biggest land mammal in the Arctic. The Arctic is a cold place at the very top of the world. The polar bear's thick fur helps to keep it warm.

The coats of some Arctic animals change colour. In winter, the Arctic hare has white fur to help hide it among the snow.

In summer its coat turns brown.

Bernie's fun facts!

The polar bear needs its thick fur to keep out the Arctic cold – even the soles of its feet are furry!

▼ Lemmings are rodents which live mostly in the cold north. They build nests under the snow in winter. During the summer, they nest underground.

The male walrus has long teeth called tusks, for digging shellfish from the seabed.

The musk ox has a long shaggy coat to help it survive the Arctic cold.

The snowshoe hare has a brown coat in summer, which turns white in winter.

▼ The leopard seal lives in the Antarctic, at the very bottom of the world. It is a fierce hunter and eats penguins, fish and even other seals. There are no land mammals in the Antarctic.

In the jungle

Jungle mammals live at all levels of the forest, from the tallest trees to the forest floor. Bats fly over the tree tops and monkeys and apes swing from branch to branch. Lower down, smaller creatures, such as civets and pottos, hide among the thick greenery.

▼ The sloth hardly ever comes down to the ground. This jungle creature hangs from a branch by its special hook-like claws.

The jaguar is one of the fiercest hunters in the jungle.

Two-toed sloth

The angwantibo has strong hands and feet for grasping branches.

▼ The okapi uses its long tongue to pick leaves from forest trees. It lives in the African rainforest.

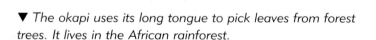

Bernie's fun facts!

The sloth spends so much time upside down that its fur grows downwards – the opposite way to most mammals. This is so that rainwater drips off more easily!

Desert life

Mammals that live in the desert have developed ways to escape the scorching heat. The North African gerbil, for example, burrows underground and only comes out at night. The fennec fox has large ears to help it lose heat.

▶ The bactrian camel has thick fur to keep it warm during the cold winters in the Gobi Desert, Asia.

Test your memory!

1. What is the biggest land mammal in the Arctic?
2. Which mammal spends most of its day in water?
3. What are a walrus's long teeth called?
4. Which mammal nests under the snow in winter?

1. the polar bear 2. the hippopotamus 3. tusks 4. the lemming

The kangaroo rat has strong back legs and can jump like a kangaroo.

The desert hedgehog eats scorpions. It nips off the deadly sting before eating.

▶ The North African gerbil is so used to desert life that it never needs to drink. It gets all the liquid it needs from its food.

The fennec fox has the largest ears for its size of any fox or dog.

City life

Foxes, rats, mice and raccoons are among the few mammals that manage to survive in towns and cities. They all eat lots of different kinds of food, so have discovered that city rubbish bins are a good, easy hunting ground.

Bernie's fun facts!

Rats will eat almost anything. They have been known to chew through electrical wires and lead piping!

The red fox
used to hunt in
the countryside
until it found
city rubbish.

Raccoons
are usually
active at night.

Rats
can live almost
anywhere, from
cupboards
to cellars.

Plant-eaters

Plant-eaters must spend much of their time eating in order to get enough nourishment (goodness from food). A zebra, for example, spends at least half its day munching grass. The good side to being a plant-eater, though, is that the animal does not have to chase and fight for its food as hunters do.

▼ Plants are the main foods for most monkeys. Some will also eat insects and other small creatures.

Rabbits have strong teeth for eating leaves and bark.

The Queensland blossom bat feeds on flower pollen and nectar.

◀ Plant-eaters, such as zebras, provide food for meat-eaters, such as lions. This is part of nature's 'food chain'.

Bernie's fun facts!

Some monkeys have a long tail which they use for climbing – like an extra arm or leg!

Hungry hunters

Mammals which hunt and kill other creatures are called carnivores. Examples of carnivores are animals such as lions, tigers, wolves and dogs. Many carnivores do not have to hunt every day – one kill will last them for several days.

▶ The tiger is the biggest of the big cats and an expert hunter. Buffalo, deer and wild pigs are its usual prey (victims).

26

Make a food chain

Make your own food chain.

1. Draw a picture of a carnivore, such as a lion, and tie it to a piece of string.

2. Draw a picture of an animal that the lion catches, such as a zebra. Hang that from the lion picture.

3. Lastly, draw some grass and plants (the food of the zebra). Hang that from the picture of the zebra.

Hunting dogs hunt in packs (groups), so that together they can kill a larger animal.

The wild boar is related to the farmyard pig. It eats plants and sometimes small animals.

The female lion (lioness) does most of the hunting for the family.

▲ Bears are carnivores, but most bears, except for the polar bear, eat more plants than meat. Brown bears eat fish, fruit, nuts and insects.

Fins and flippers

Most swimming mammals have flippers and fins instead of legs. Seals and sea lions have paddle-like flippers. They use them to drag themselves along on land, as well as for swimming in water. Whales never come to land. They swim by moving their tails up and down and using their front flippers to steer.

Bowhead whale

Killer whale

▶ The Weddell seal can dive deeper than any other seal.

Narwhal

► The harp seal lives in the Arctic Ocean.

► The northern fur seal has larger rear flippers than other fur seals.

The bowhead whale uses filters in its mouth to catch food.

The narwhal has a long tooth growing out from its lip.

The killer whale is the largest member of the dolphin family.

Test your memory!

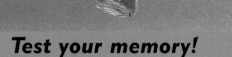

1. What is the name of animals that eat meat?
2. Which small mammal can eat almost anything?
3. What does the Queensland blossom bat eat?
4. Which mammal is the wild boar related to?

4. the pig
1. carnivores 2. the rat 3. flower pollen and nectar

Champion diggers

The burrowing experts of the mammal world are prairie dogs. These little animals are not dogs at all but a kind of plump, short-tailed squirrel. They live in large burrows, which contain several chambers linked by tunnels.

The volcano rabbit digs burrows for shelter on the slopes of volcanoes.

The ground squirrel has strong front paws to help it dig underground.

▲ Badgers dig a network of chambers and tunnels called a sett. They usually stay in their setts during the day and come cut at night.

▲ The mole has special front feet for digging. It has poor eyesight but a good sense of touch.

Bernie's fun facts!

Badgers are playful animals – the adults are often seen enjoying a good game of leapfrog with their cubs!

Staying safe

Some animals have special ways of defending themselves from enemies. The nine-banded armadillo protects itself with its body armour. The porcupine's body is covered with sharp spines. The skunk defends itself with a bad-smelling fluid.

▲ *This creature is called a pangolin. Its body is covered by tough scales. These protect it from the bites of insects, its favourite food.*

▲ *The nine-banded armadillo is covered with strong, bony plates.*

The skunk lifts its tail and sprays its enemy with smelly fluid, then runs away.

The porcupine will run towards its attacker and stick the spines into its flesh.

Bernie's fun facts!

Smelly skunks sometimes feed on bees. They roll the bees on the ground to remove their stings before eating them.

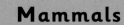

▲ The rhinoceros may charge its enemies at top speed. Rhinoceroses are generally peaceful animals, but a female will defend her young fiercely.

Best builders

Beavers build special homes made from sticks, stones and mud. They start by blocking a stream to create a dam, or wall. They then build a shelter, called a lodge. This is usually a dome-shaped structure made of sticks and mud.

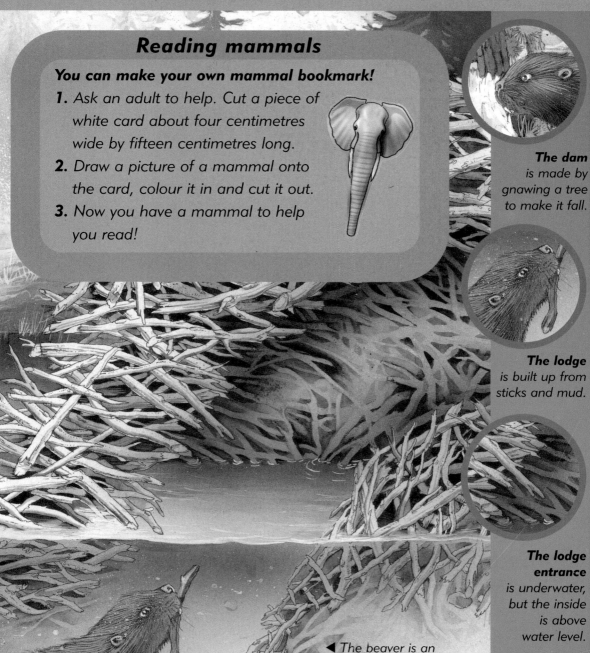

Reading mammals

You can make your own mammal bookmark!

1. Ask an adult to help. Cut a piece of white card about four centimetres wide by fifteen centimetres long.

2. Draw a picture of a mammal onto the card, colour it in and cut it out.

3. Now you have a mammal to help you read!

The dam is made by gnawing a tree to make it fall.

The lodge is built up from sticks and mud.

The lodge entrance is underwater, but the inside is above water level.

◀ The beaver is an excellent swimmer. It has webbed feet and a flat tail which act like paddles.

Getting at food

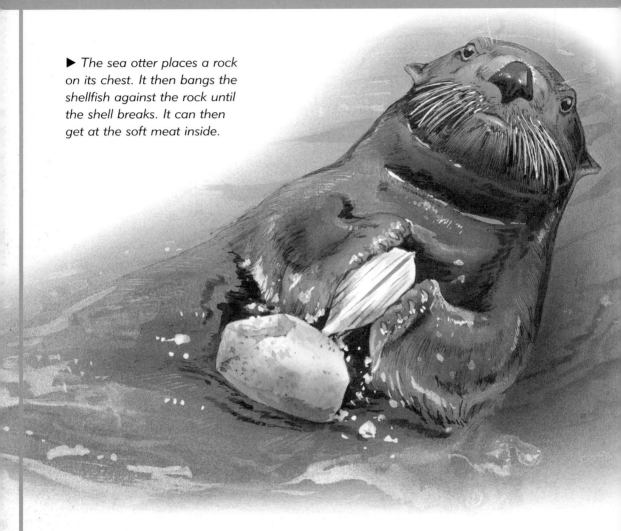

▶ The sea otter places a rock on its chest. It then bangs the shellfish against the rock until the shell breaks. It can then get at the soft meat inside.

Some mammals use tools to help them find food. The chimpanzee uses a stone as a hammer to crack nuts, and sticks to help catch insects. The sea otter uses a stone to break open shellfish.

36

▼ The chimp pokes a sharp stick into a termite or ant nest. It waits a moment then pulls the stick out, covered with insects for the chimp to eat.

Squirrels use their front paws to turn their food as they eat.

The giraffe has a long tongue to pull leaves within reach.

Bernie's fun facts!

A mammal called a cusimanse knows how to get at the tasty insides of an egg – by smashing it open against a tree!

Baby mammals

Female mammals feed their young on the milk they produce. Some young mammals, such as antelopes, have to be up and running less than an hour after birth or they will be killed by predators (hunters).

Other mammals, such as rabbits, are born blind and helpless.

Test your memory!

1. Which mammal is the largest member of the dolphin family?

2. What is the name for the tunnels that badgers dig?

3. What is the shelter built by beavers called?

4. Which animal is a good digger but has bad eyesight?

1. the killer whale 2. a sett 3. a lodge 4. the mole

The Virginia opossum has more babies than any other mammal – as many as 21.

The elephant has the longest pregnancy of any mammal – about twenty months.

◄ The female puma, or mountain lion, gives birth to cubs (babies) with spotted fur. The spots disappear as the cubs grow older.

A baby panda stays with its mother for up to two years.

Index

A B
angwantibo 18, **19**
Arctic and Antarctic
 16, 17
armadillo, nine-banded
 32
baby mammals **6–7**,
 38–39
baboon, olive **6**
badger **31**
bat **5**, **7**, 12, 18
 fruit-eating **13**
 hog-nosed 8, **9**
 Queensland blossom
 25
 vampire **13**
bear 7, **8**, **27**
beaver **4**, **34–35**
boar, wild **27**

C D
camel, bactrian **20**
capybara **9**
carnivores (meat-eaters)
 25, **26–27**
cheetah **4**, **10–11**
chimp/chimpanzee 8,
 36, **37**
cusimanse 37
deer 7
 fallow **7**
 mouse **9**
dog, hunting **27**
dolphin, Ganges
 15

E F G
echidna **7**
eggs 7
elephant **4**, **8**, **39**
food chain 25, 27
fox 22
 fennec 20, 21
 red **22**, **23**
fur 16, 20
gerbil, North African
 20, **21**
giraffe **9**, **37**
glider **12**
gorilla **8**

H J K
hare
 Arctic 16
 snowshoe **17**
 brown 10, **11**
hedgehog, desert **21**
hippo/hippopotamus
 14, **15**
humans 4, 8, **9**
jaguar **18**, **19**
kangaroo **7**, **11**
killer whale **28**, **29**

L M N
lemming **17**
lemur, flying **12–13**
lion **4**, 26, 27
lodge **34**, **35**
manatee **15**
marsupials 7

meerkat **4**, **5**
milk 38
mole **31**
monkey **18**, **25**
narwhal **29**

O P
okapi **19**
opossum **15**, **39**
otter
 Eurasian (river) **4**,
 5, **14**
 sea **36**
ox, musk **17**
panda **39**
pangolin **32**
placenta **6**
plant-eaters **24–25**
platypus **15**
polar bear **16**
porcupine 32, **33**
pouch (marsupial) 7
prairie dog **30**
primates 8
pronghorn 10, **11**
puma **38–39**

R S
rabbit **25**, 38
 volcano **31**
raccoon 22, **23**
rat **22**, **23**
 kangaroo **21**
 water 14, **15**
rhino/rhinoceros **33**

rodents 9, 17
seal 28
 harp **29**
 leopard **17**
 northern fur **29**
 Weddell **28**
sett **31**
shrew, pygmy **9**
skunk 32, **33**
sloth **19**
squirrel 37
 flying **12–13**
 ground **31**

T W Z
tarsier, Western **5**
tiger **26**
tools **36–37**
tusks **17**
walrus **17**
warm-blooded 4
whale 28
 blue **8–9**
 bowhead **28–29**
zebra **24–25**